'UNDER CONSTRUCTION'
FROM THE FIRST BALL TO
THE LAST BALL

23/06/19

MARIETTA,
WE ARE All
UNDER CONSTRUCTION,
YOUR JOURNEY IN
Life PROVES THAT
HARD WORK IS
COURAGE UNLEASHED.

HAPPY Birthday,
Anthony

Cover design and book publication by EPCO Communications
Cover illustration by Shane Logan
Graphics – Bob Davis

ISBN # 0-9660315-9-8

NICK BOLLETTIERI

'UNDER CONSTRUCTION'
FROM THE FIRST BALL TO
THE LAST BALL

WRITTEN BY:
NICK BOLLETTIERI AND
ANTHONY C. GRUPPO

WARNING: This book may be hazardous to your personality if you suffer
from extreme needs for structure, order, or detail, and may encourage motivation
and leadership abilities resulting in a free-thinking visionary.

–The Authors

"UNDER CONSTRUCTION" – FROM THE FIRST BALL TO THE LAST BALL

INTRODUCTION

"Under Construction" connects us together whether our life experiences come from the boardroom, family room or locker room. Regardless of our personal arena, we are all players in the same game. Whether we are eight or eighty, every day we choose our opportunities by our first and last ball.

In this book, you may see yourself in my stories and experiences. It is an invitation to share in my life's construction and then together achieve our personal potential. I refuse to pretend to have the answers, rather I have chosen to identify the construction sites of life and the materials necessary to engage your personal first and last balls.

My book listens more than it speaks. It has listened to all the people who have made my personal construction process both exciting and challenging. I invite you to read this book and hear its many voices. I believe you will feel part of these first and last balls because we are all workers on the same construction site of life.

My intention is not to be a motivational preacher, but rather an experienced architect in constructing personal potential.

Everyone is constantly under construction. Life is a series of first and last balls. *"Under Construction"* offers you, the reader, thoughts and concepts to consider in constructing your success.

"Under Construction" will assist you in achieving your complete potential. It is not a book that defines success; it is a collection of experiences to guide you to your personal potential and abilities.

Nick Bollettieri

TABLE OF CONTENTS

PREFACE

PREFACE

I parked the rental car in the lot of the Bollettieri Sports Academy. I looked at the face of my son Anthony Jr., you would have thought that I had brought him to the most magical place on earth. He looked at me and said, "Thank you Dad for letting me come here for the week." Little did I realize that it was I who would be thanking him. Because of Anthony's passion for tennis I was about to meet a great leader, Nick Bollettieri.

I sat in the stands at the front court of the Academy. Nick was coaching and instructing Serena Williams. Everyone seemed to be watching Serena. I was watching Nick. I found myself concentrating on his delivery and manner. It was clear that he was a general directing his troops. There was little doubt who was in charge.

I stood up and informed my family that it was time I introduced myself to Nick Bollettieri. I thought I heard a sigh of concern from Anthony Jr., as I left the stands. Nick was leaving the court with a staff person, asking his opinion on a document. There is always anxiety when you are about to meet someone famous. That all disappeared when we shook hands. I knew this handshake. It was the handshake of a man that focused on who he was meeting. A leader who always made time to meet someone who had taken the time to meet him.

Anthony Jr., had a wonderful week at the Academy. Everyday he thanked me for the opportunity. My family has vacationed in some of the most beautiful places on earth however I now saw in Anthony Jr's eyes that they would all be second to his time at the Academy. Each day, Nick was there with his players working in the intense August heat. He always seemed fresh and ready to achieve. There was the sensation I felt watching him work, that he did not coach only his players to achieve, he was there; after all his successful years, still setting new goals for himself. Believe me, I could smell the scent of leadership from the stands.

As an advocate of children and families in crisis, the atmosphere of the Academy fascinated me. I saw in the coaches and staff the same dedication and passion I see in child-care professionals. Nick has been kind enough to allow me to share a few of my thoughts in this book. He believes that making the connection between sports, business, children and families is important. He understands that leadership is taking our primary skill package and developing it to our full potential.

If you would simply consider our thoughts and experiences, you may view your life differently. When a player leaves a coach, a client leaves a professional, or a child leaves a family, it is usually because the mentor asked the student to make the difficult choice. For Nick Bollettieri to be remembered simply as a world famous tennis coach is a tragedy. He should be remembered as a spirit of humanity. He always had his vision and focus set to achieve the difficult. If he asked that of others, it is because he demanded it of himself. And isn't that the definition of a leader?

For I truly believe that Nick Bollettieri placed titanium in the hearts and minds of his players long before the manufacturers placed it in their racquets. Regardless of your role in life, you the reader have an opportunity to learn these lessons that will allow you to play on any surface which life asks you to stand. If you follow the coach, you will be victorious over the toughest challenger you will ever face—Yourself!

Anthony C. Gruppo

1

THE FIRST BALL

THE FIRST BALL

Mr. Agassi took great delight in showing me how he placed a ball above the cot and watched Andre swing for the first time. Likewise, I recently remember my daughter Nicole, tell me she couldn't wait to get her driving license so she could ride in the car without me.

Tommy Haas asked me, "Nick, when do I volley?" I said, "Tommy, start out by volleying all the time and you will find the answer to your question." By volleying all the time, Tommy discovered two other insights into the First Ball- where to volley and why. Taking advantage of the " First Ball" is one thing. Knowing where to hit it is another.

There is a special mystique that accompanies the "First Ball". I can still remember Martina Hingis, at only eleven years of age, playing the Girls eighteen's at the Junior French Open. Even though she was so young to be playing this event, I knew right then and there that she knew the trick of the game. She knew it starts with the "First Ball".

Life has rewarded me because I have made a habit of getting the most out of every First Ball.

Seven years later, in November 1998, Martina and her mother trained at our Academy for two weeks. The objective to be accomplished was the very same as it was when she was eleven- the "First Ball".

On November 22, 1998, I flew to New York to watch Martina play Lindsey Davenport for the WTA World's Championship. She won in four sets that day. Without saying a word, Martina, her mother and I all knew why. Martina had once again regained that special ingredient- the "First Ball".

Life has taught me to cherish the "First Ball". I view each "First Ball" as an opportunity to test my ability. Tennis, like life rewards those of us who make a habit of taking the "First Ball" all the time. I do not fear the results; I simply accept the challenge.

2

GROWTH SPURT

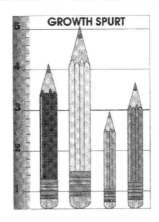

GROWTH SPURT

Can you believe that at my age I still have growth spurts? I do and they are always welcomed. A personal and professional growth spurt is a reminder that we are accepting new challenges and creating exciting opportunities. A professional growth spurt builds confidence and character. There have been many temptations in my life to slow down and rest on my reputation and fame. I have refused them all; the loss of my treasured growth spurts would be missed beyond belief.

**A professional growth spurt is the movement
from the ordinary to the extraordinary.
We can see the new edge to achieve the impossible.**

I have often been asked this simple question; "Nick, which would you select: The most talented player with a poor work ethic and no sense of responsibility or a less talented player with the determination to succeed that is second to none? I will always choose the less talented player with a superior work ethic. Those players constantly have growth spurts, which enable them to grow as a person and a player.

Unfortunately, many professional athletes act as if the world owes them something special because they have talent. They may continue to grow as a player, but without personal growth spurts they die as a person. They rob themselves of the reward they

7

would gain through their service to humanity. I do not speak from some high personal podium; I speak from mistakes and the tuition life charges those that consider themselves superior to others. While building my profession, there were times when I chose my players over opportunities with my children. While my children were having their growth spurts, I was with my players having my own spurt to build a quality of life for my family. The tuition charge was lost time with my family.

All professionals that travel from home pay the same tuition. We struggle from the need to create professional growth spurts and the love of precious time with our loved ones. I believe we can have both. Our families need to witness the growth spurts we have in our adult lives. It prepares the children to accept responsibility and give back to society when their talents are rewarded with blessings.

Visionaries, thinkers and leaders crave personal and professional growth spurts. They are able to move quickly to the challenges available to the person in the lead. To grow is to accept the risk that accompanies the unknown. From the locker room to the family room, the need to grow is the essence for creativity. Wherever our path leads us, we should look at personal and professional growth spurts as the fuel to seek new heights. As for Nick Bollettieri, *I do not stay because of the success of yesterday or the thrill of today. I continue to stay for the dreams of tomorrow.*

3

UNDER CONSTRUCTION

UNDER CONSTRUCTION

**If we keep our surface under construction, we will build
the endurance to reach personal potential. Responsibility
will forever become our Partner to achievement.**

We should constantly take the responsibility to change the surface we know and compete on the surface of life that is unknown. Often, people try to stick to what they do best in order to maintain a consistent responsibility. Responsibility can always be smoothed over if it never changes. Our responsibility is rarely challenged if the routine is always the same.

On June 4, 1998, I wrote a letter to Nick Philippoussis, the father of my then student Mark Philippoussis. I believed that Mark needed to change his "surface". Mark is a big man with a big serve. I knew that the "surface" of power was not enough to bring him to his full potential. I established a plan for Mark that called for serious thought to building points, games, sets and matches. I wanted Mark to take responsibility and move beyond his comfort zone of power. He needed to attack short balls, chip and charge, and attack the net. I felt my suggestions were not being considered so we decided to part company.

On September 12, 1998, Mark competed in the semi-finals of the US Open against Carlos Moya. In an exciting match, he defeated Moya. He served and volleyed, chipped and charged. I felt as though my June letter was a screenplay being acted out on

11

television. Mark had learned to take responsibility and change his "surface". When he placed his "surface" under construction, he gained the endurance to achieve to a new level. He hired responsibility as a partner to achievement.

Endurance serves only one master. It serves the person with the ability to focus and blast through the fatigue of change. Physical training is not sufficient to produce the endurance necessary to be victorious. It also comes from the heart and passion to push through pain and pressure. The person standing will be the one that can dig deep into their reservoir of strength and accept the responsibility to change their "surface".

The individual that learns to compete on multiple surfaces has the greatest opportunity for success. We, like the advice I gave to Mark, need an aggressive style of play to offset the bad bounce. We can never afford to sit on life's baseline hoping for the big break.

Accept the responsibility to learn a new surface. Have the courage to challenge yourself. Let no one stand in your way of achieving beyond your talent. Establish a level of endurance that carries you through the pressure of the unknown. The surface you thought would be difficult is always easier when you accept the responsibility and fight for your dreams.

4

CRADLES AND KENNELS

CRADLES AND KENNELS

It's amazing how despite our faults as parents; our children have the ability to continue to love us. In spite of the abuse and neglect dogs suffer for being lower on the great chain of being, they still wag their tails when we come through the door. Tolerance seems so natural for them. We all start with it, yet we often lose it and have to search through the rubble before it's regained.

Tolerance can take a while, but what a difference it makes in our lives. It can for anyone, if you're willing to accept that it's absolute. Once you concede to it's absoluteness, life isn't nearly as difficult or as complicated as it once seemed.

Danielle's Dogs
It would be a stretch to say that I have been the best father, but yet my oldest daughter, Danielle, loves me without qualification. Why? Let's just say that there is one thing that Danielle loves more than her father....her dogs.

If this sounds tainted with jealousy, forgive me. After all, her dogs are not what you might expect. That is, they are not gorgeous thoroughbreds with prized names like Count Hessian III or King Basel of Prussia, whose proud lineage extends back through history. On the contrary, her dogs are the dregs of the dog world. These lost and emaciated mongrels find their way onto the property and into Danielle's heart. Yes, Danielle is the Mother Theresa of the dog world and the word is out. If you're lost, alone, hungry, diseased, and abused, present yourself to Danielle.

You don't have to be a dog person to be an observer of their behavior. Danielle's office is next to mine and yes, you guessed it, her dogs, often as many as three or four, accompany her to work each day. The dogs are not particularly well behaved and have the run of the executive office. What can I say? I love my daughter and if the dogs despite their disruptions make her happy, then I'm happy.

Dog lovers will tell you that dogs are beautiful, loyal, intelligent, empathetic, and, of course, life long friends. All of which, judging from their extraordinary behavior, would seem to be true. For others, a dog is just a dog, unsuited to human traits. That doesn't make them any less lovable. It just makes them dogs.

Regardless of your affection for dogs, the one characteristic they have more of than some humans is tolerance.

Tolerance, if anything, is what best characterizes dogs. Abuse them, violate them, betray them, misapply them, malign them, assail them, denounce them, disparage them and even insult them, they will still be happy to see you. Now, that's tolerance and thank God that is what Danielle's dogs have taught her. A lesson Danielle, in her gift of love, has handed me.

No one is more thankful than I am for what dogs teach us. I believe this is why, despite my faults, she still loves me. Danielle, thank you for being tolerant of a cantankerous old man.

16

S.P.C.A. for Kids

As sad as it sounds when dogs are mistreated, the same can be said of children. Particularly children in the foster care system. These kids are abused, violated, betrayed, insulted and displaced from their families. Sometimes it seems they are members of their own S.P.C.A., the Special Problem Children of America. It is easier to find good homes for dogs, than it is to find good homes for foster kids.

No matter how poorly they were treated by their families, they still hope to go home. They are shuffled from one foster home to another and look forward to the day that Mom or Dad is well enough to take them home. Often treated like strays, shouldn't we be more tolerant of kids when they keep bouncing back and waiting for us to care? We all deserve guidance, understanding, and protection.

**If we can make room for our own ups and downs,
we should always make room for theirs.**

Stray Tolerance

Tolerance says it loud and clear. Now, there's a virtue we could all capitalize on in our personal relationships, people we work with, people we will know, and people we'll never know. We'd like to think that tolerance cannot be quantified. Consider the dogs. Remember the children. There is no partial tolerance in their nature. If they can bring it upon themselves to give tolerance without condition, then surely we as adult humans, the role models and supposed pinnacle of evolution, can do so equally.

17

Embrace tolerance and the deep prejudices that surround everything from skin color, to religion, to nationality, will melt away. Embrace tolerance and you free yourself of petty burdens, which are usually couched in fear.

Whether, it's the S.P.C.A. strays or the Special Problem Children of America, it's a lesson well learned. We can do no better than to model the strays and displaced children of the world by approaching others with the same respect and tolerance they show us. Our hope being that in your wisdom you will pass it on to all you encounter and realize the return is even greater. Do this and you will never look at strays of any kind the same way again!

5

TAKE A KNEE

TAKE A KNEE

It always bothers me when an adult speaks to a child and doesn't have the common sense to take a knee and speak to them at eye level. So many people speak to children instead of with children. But, I suppose it should be no surprise that they are the same to their colleagues at work. I know executives that their living room is like a boardroom. Better their kids come downstairs with a briefcase instead of a Lego set.

These are the same executives that complain that they have no time for their families because of their demanding schedule. They actually use e-mail on their laptops to communicate with their children from the road. Then, when their child doesn't act exactly as they believe they should, the child is placed on behavioral medication. No surprise we sold more Prozac than Tylenol in this country last year.

I love to spend time with the young children that come to the Academy. For some, their racquets are longer than their legs. They all are eager to learn and play. I have a teaching technique where I ask them to form a straight line across the court. I stand in the middle of the line and together we walk to the net discussing the theory of the game. I wonder how many parents take the time to walk with children and discuss the game of life?

We must mentor the young children. In return, they will assist us to remember how to communicate with our inner child.

There would be time for children if we applied time management skills at work and playtime skills at home. We think nothing of harping about our personal lives for an hour at the office. Instead of concentrating on work and being home an hour earlier at night.

Our nation's children's homes are filled with kids labeled as behavioral problems. Their parents can't handle them at home. But, many of these kids received no attention or love in the home. They begin to act out to signal their frustration of being ignored. Same problem in the workplace. The leader is so worried about their own career they fail to mentor those around them. Eventually, corporate renegades develop and chaos follows.

The title of parent is much more important than the one on a business card. Get rid of that business card title. If we stop measuring each other by a title, perhaps we will stop putting titles on our kids. Let them play and find time to play with them. In the end, you will be more successful at work because you will stop taking yourself so seriously. Have you ever played army with a child? They never get hit. They always find a way to survive. We can all take a lesson from that. So, take a knee and pay attention.

6

FEAR OF THE UNKNOWN

FEAR OF THE UNKNOWN

The solution came to me late one summer evening. At the time, the Academy was located at the Colony Beach Resort on Longboat Key, which for those unfamiliar is situated on the shores of Florida's Gulf coast. We had just finished several hours of hard work on the courts. The kids and the pros were exhausted. I had promised that if they were prepared to end their day with some physical conditioning on the beach, everyone was free to go to the movies.

The vision of them racing along the beach in a glorious celebration of youth and energy made me feel proud of the kids and immensely satisfied with our efforts. With one last look at the setting sun, I turned to leave when I realized that the waves were cresting a foot or two higher than normal. Spring tides I thought to myself. Not wanting to miss the occasion, headed for my room, grabbed my surfboard, and made my way out to just beyond the cresting waves.

For those of you who have never surfed, surfing is not so much about taming the waves. In the end, the waves always win. Surfing is about working with the waves, about doing what you do well, and allowing the wave's grace and power to complement your abilities. I guess I always knew this, but it wasn't until this particular late afternoon while lying on my board and allowing the wave's rhythms to cleanse the day's efforts that I fully realized the parallel to my own life. Like most thoughts of clarity, they came to me not in a flash of understanding, but in pieces. The sum of the pieces became so clear.

25

I rode the next wave back to the beach with the new realization that while not as talented as some of the people I had hired, a great leader hires themselves everyday for the toughest position in the game.

The position of a visionary is on the edge carrying colleagues to the new game against the best opponent.

Some athletes refuse to compete against a much better opponent. There are parents who are afraid to let their children attempt a difficult task because they may fail. There are executives that will not explore new markets for fear that they may not have the talent to lead. Many fear what they do not understand. This fear for them is a wake-up call. If we do not allow the talent of others to rise, there will be no wave to ride.

I determined a new course for my coworkers and myself. From that day on, I vowed to work as I had done with my surfing – with the wave's grace and strength. I would hold my edges to the best of my ability and expect nothing less from the wave. Where I could, I would mold and cut the wave and where the wave had strength, I would concede to its freedom. That is how I've conducted my business life ever since. Without fear, I've surrounded myself with the brightest and the best and it is they that have made the difference. Myself charged by their talent and dedication and them spurred with my energy and passion. We ride the crest of every wave.

Work in tandem allowing the wave and its strength to assure you that you will always make it back to shore. Trust in the wave and its ability to sustain you. In a world buffeted by unpredictability and fear, you will be forever steady in riding the waves of your disappointments and successes.

7

WELCOME TO
NEVER-NEVER LAND

WELCOME TO NEVER-NEVER LAND

N ever- Never Land really does exist; it exists when you believe that you are stuck with no way to achieve your goals.

Our childhood memories can create our adult dreams.

Always believe in your ability. Believe that you will succeed in your attempt to challenge the unknown. Never be afraid to try new things. In the story, Peter Pan and Captain Hook tried everything to defeat each other. They lived and battled on Never-Never Land. Captain Hook could never defeat Peter Pan. I believe that is why they called it Never- Never Land because Captain Hook was never going to win.

You can use the same techniques as Pan did in your competitions. Peter never underestimated his ability to fight the pirates even though they had him outnumbered. He always thought he would succeed with his plan. He would try new things with the Lost Boys to stop Hook. And, if Hook temporarily got the upper hand, he always stayed positive.

Peter Pan may be fictional, but his plan is very real. Today, some of our greatest sports champions act like Peter Pan. They have the ability to fly like Peter Pan over the court, field or track. They believe in their ability to win. Even if they are hurt or up against a tougher opponent, they still believe in their ability. They constantly learn new plays and drills to improve their skills. When they do lose a game or a match, they believe they can return and win the next time.

In your life, you can achieve what you dream. If your dream is to be a great tennis player, hard work will get you to your dream. If you desire to be a good student, study hard and you will be successful. All we need is the Peter Pan Plan. The plan may seem tough, but it is really very simple.

First, never believe someone else when they say you will fail. If you try new things, regardless of the outcome you have already won. Second, always trust in your ability to succeed in accomplishing your goals. Third, if you lose in your attempt, stay positive and try again.

All the great champions fail at something in their life. But, they refuse to live in Never-Never Land. Have confidence in your ability and continue to reach your goals and dreams. For you, Never- Never Land will never exist.

8

THE COMMON OVERHEAD

THE COMMON OVERHEAD

Think about all the organizations that use the overhead slide to communicate their visions and corporate messages. Organizations use electronic or plastic slide programs to share their mission and strategy with the audience. The presenter is vulnerable during their presentation because they are taking risks by showing the audience their concepts and ideas on the overhead screen.

The overhead shot in tennis follows the same techniques as the overhead in business. A tennis player knows that they hit the overhead when they are on the most vulnerable spot on the court. The player realizes that they are taking a risk by hitting the shot. Any mistake in hitting the overhead will result in disaster.

A player understands that after they hit an overhead they must attack the net. This attack will prevent the opponent from recovering successfully. In business, the designer and creator of company ideas is like the tennis player with the overhead shot. They should see the entire business- playing surface and move their opponent to the most difficult spot to defend. The business professional attacks the marketplace just as a tennis player attacks the net.

When I coach my players on the overhead, I remind them of these three points. First, remember that the overhead is risky. When hitting the overhead, the player stands in no man's land on the court. Second, you cannot be afraid to take this risk because a successful overhead will win points. Third, after hitting the shot, attack the net and gain the advantage over your opponent.

The same strategy can serve to help the corporate planner. When you are preparing the business strategy that you will be presenting to your colleagues, remember my advice to players. Concentrate on the overheads that contain your vision; remember you are a risk-taker. Present your programs and ideas and attack the marketplace. The key in hitting a successful overhead shot is to look up at the ball and challenge yourself. The same is true in business. Look ahead to your goals and challenge the future.

When making your presentation, trust your instincts. Take a risk and find a reward. Challenge yourself to accomplish goals in the most difficult business arenas. You can achieve the dream that soars overhead. Look up, focus on the target, and hit your best shot. Leaders know the reward was well worth the risk.

9

RETURN OF SERVE

RETURN OF SERVE

L ook at the eyes of the players as they prepare to return serve. If they think, blink or flinch, it's all over. Players know that they must pick up the ball immediately, react, and produce a compact swing.

Look at the eyes of business professionals as they prepare to return serve. The professional should anticipate the issues, react to them quickly, and produce service in a streamlined and efficient delivery.

Look at the eyes of parents as they prepare to return serve. They return serve just like players and professionals. Their skills must be up to the power and strength of the server. They quickly assess the needs of their family, react to the problems in society that endanger their children, and raise loving, happy, and successful adults.

Look at your own eyes. Are you ready to return the serves in your life? If you make solid and timely decisions, react to your opportunities and stay motivated, you will never be aced. We all have our faults, but with correct adjustments there will be few doubles.

10

SEEING DOUBLES

SEEING DOUBLES

A doubles match is the essence of teamwork. The players need to know how their partner will react in game situations. They learn how to cover for each other. They communicate during the match and motivate their partner to achieve victory. They conceive a strategic plan to dominate their opponents. They are a partnership focused on success.

Watching a doubles team is an excellent model for family and business. Parents are a doubles team that understands how they react when challenged. They use their individual strengths to secure the team. They must communicate their thoughts and fears in order to bring their family to success. They develop a plan to raise children to find success and happiness.

Mark Knowles came to the Bollettieri Academy when he was ten years old. In spite of his hard work, he struggled as a singles player. Mark used his strength as a team player and became one of the most successful doubles players in the world.

In business, some professionals struggle to succeed as a solo performer. When placed on a team, they achieve because of the support and structure. Having a partner enhances their motivation and focus.

On the court and in life, we often hear more about the individual. The doubles team at home and at work is the foundation for success. All leaders know that their future rests on the team. Find your partner and charge the net to victory.

11

THE BROKEN STRING

THE BROKEN STRING

The racquets manufactured today are fantastic. They are powerful, lightweight, and practically indestructible. However, if you break a string, they are rendered useless. A player would never consider going to a match with only one racquet. Without the safeguard of several racquets, success for the player is in jeopardy.

In business, the employees are the strings of the organization. The corporation may have a strong financial frame and an oversized product arsenal. However, should tension exist among the employees, a string can snap and render the company useless. Just like the tension of a racquet, an unhealthy company will produce internal tension.

Corporations need quality employees to deliver their best game. Leaders should always give credit to the people that helped make them successful. This keeps the tension low and the productivity high.

Perhaps you are a business professional that enjoys the game of tennis. Take a look at your tennis racquet. Compare the grip to your company's hold on the marketplace. The oversized head can relate to the expansion of your services. View your strings as the people that support your mission and vision. One broken string could force you from the competition.

12

THE STOP WATCH

THE STOP WATCH

S top your watch and start your dreams. I do not wear a watch and I never miss an appointment. I have not worn a watch for many years because watching time prevents focus and attention to the task. Checking the time is a distraction and breaks the concentration needed to achieve goals. For the leader, goal setting and achievement should be twenty-four hours a day and seven days a week. Even when at play, my mind is always planning and establishing the next leap to a new challenge.

Take a moment and pay attention to how many times in the course of the day you look at your watch. We often hesitate, looking at the time and waiting for something to begin or end. The watch for many is more than a timepiece; it has become a distraction from the focus of the goal.

Often, we time our events. We watch the time to leave for an appointment or use it to make an excuse to escape from a person or place. When surprised by an unexpected event, we can use our watch to plan our retreat.

Leaders never measure time in minutes.
For them, time is measured in goals per minute.
Consider stopping your watch and starting your dreams.
Clock your time in goals.

51

Look at young people prior to the age of sixteen. Rarely, do you see them wearing a watch. They focus on play or the project until they are finished or bored. We can all learn from the children. Never allow time to dictate results or performance. Watching time is a distraction from achieving successful results.

When I stand on the court teaching, time is both my energy and enemy. Time can be my energy because I have so much I want to give my student. I pay no attention to the clock or the length of time we have been working. Together, we work for the time we will be leaders and not the time of day. Time is my enemy because as the clock ticks away I have so many dreams to still fulfill.

Time management begins with the absence of time watching. Manage your timing to opportunity and focus on one goal at a time. Time is energy to the leader because it starts fresh every day. We can stop time through our success. In the future, others will measure time against our clock. The clock of the leader never needs to be reset.

13

STAND AND DELIVER

STAND AND DELIVER

I have what most would consider a traditional office. At the Bollettieri Sports Academy, I maintain an office where our staff conducts our business operations. I believe, however, my true office is wherever I stand. Most of my working day is spent standing on the courts, delivering to the best of my ability for my players, coaches and colleagues. My office never has been a desk, chair or file cabinet. The office of Nick Bollettieri is where I stand and deliver.

Working while standing allows us to be more energetic and animated. Life is a stage, so never sit for your performance. Watching the energy of my players is a lifeline to my personal delivery system. The office where I stand is a court filled with motion and emotion. The players and coaches are caught up in the creation and delivery of potential. I believe that is why I never become tired of the process. There is energy generated in a stand-up office.

There are those that marvel at my energy level. There is so much energy wasted in the traditional office setting. Before an executive can begin working, there is a great amount of energy wasted before the performance begins. Meetings, discussions, memos and mail all deplete energy. I walk onto the court; stand and deliver. We all can increase our energy and reduce the traditional hold placed on us by the standard office.

**We deliver our mission from the stage of life.
Remember to stand and deliver your performance.**

Create for yourself a stand-up office. When you enter your office tomorrow, remove your chair completely from the room. Give your chair to a colleague who is currently using the standard issued staff chair. Morale will increase and others will wonder what you are doing. Place a platform on your desk that raises your work area above waist height. Speak and write from a standing position. You will notice a vast difference in your phone techniques. There will be better concentration and listening skills when handling a call from a colleague or client. Those that interrupt you will not stay long in your office because you are already standing. It sends a signal that you are focused and in no mood for a social chitchat.

We can all stand and deliver. Tradition, be it process or position, is a thief of our energy. A physical office transformation from a seat to your feet is a signal that you plan to be standing when you greet your future.

There are times that I sit at my desk. I have been told I appear to be a lion chained to a wall. There are meetings I must attend and mail I must read. That is process not performance delivery. When you awake and stand up tomorrow, remain standing and deliver your mission with energy and animation. You are a tremendous performer. Now, prepare to give yourself a standing ovation.

14

ON THE RUN

ON THE RUN

Mark McGwire completes his magical run at the home run record and hits number 62. At the same time at the 98' US Open, a tennis player runs down a return to make an impossible shot. The crowd at both events cheers with excitement and marvels at the achievement. For a brief moment, the spectator is one with the performer on their run. When we witness an incredible feat, we all become fans of the sport; if only for the moment.

Speed is a great weapon for the tennis player. It allows them to overcome a weak return and steal the thunder from their opponent's apparent winner. Speed can change the momentum and break the opposition's spirit. When faced with speed, the player knows they should play their best game. The angles become ever more important to neutralize the faster player.

All the great speed artists realize they only rent their gift. In time, their speed will dissolve with age. They all know that even within their prime lease of speed, there is always someone faster. Whether it is the deadline to speed to a homerun record or the speed to run down a shot, time is critical. More pressure exists for the fast; they may have less time to achieve.

We all should become faster. In business, we must have speed to market for products and services. In our homes, we should run to gain the advantage for our children. We are all on a short time frame to achieve a better life for ourselves and those we care about. We should all purchase the proper foot"where" for the race. We need to know that where we are standing is always the start of the race. Today, look where you are and make a fast dash to your future.

15

CAN YOU SPARE SOME CHANGE?

CAN YOU SPARE SOME CHANGE?

I continue to be amazed at the amount of corporate money spent on change management consultants. Where I come from, you either change or disappear. Every day, I ask my players and coaches to change whatever is necessary to achieve to their full potential.

If tomorrow I decided to come to the courts at 9:00a.m. instead of my usual 6:45a.m, I believe no one would question the change. People may rationalize that after all these years of coaching the great players I deserve the break. Never will I do that because it is my work ethic that drives my ability to change. We should all realize that a hard charging work ethic is the platform where change is launched to seek new and greater success.

Why do we fear change? I truly fear the absence of change. Without change, there is no growth.

It applies in the world of sport or business. As a coach, I constantly push our players to separate what they know and experiment with the opportunity to learn the unknown. The blending of their familiar skill package with the experimental skills being developed creates a leader.

In the early years, I focused on the skills necessary to be a tennis coach. Later, it became critical that I learn the skills necessary to be a successful businessperson. I have had more failures than successes. I consider the failures to be learning experiences and far more valuable than the success.

Failure is the ticket to the game and success is the scoreboard.

Can you spare some change? Of course you can, if you embrace change as your path to achievement. Change is your blueprint to construct a winner in life. The fear of change is usually much greater than the result of the change. Regardless of your role in life, you can become a visionary. A visionary knows that change is both coach and motivator. Others will follow the changes you create. A visionary sees life on the edge because that is where change has its greatest reward.

Tomorrow brings opportunity if we change the way we attacked yesterday. We must not reach a comfort zone that makes us fearful of change. I discovered many years ago that worrying about the past froze my ability to succeed in the future. Forward movement is the greatest icebreaker to achieve your goals.

16

WEATHER IT OUT

WEATHER IT OUT

It is amazing to watch what happens during a rain delay at a tournament. Everyone begins to question how the players will react. What effect will the delay have on the veteran as compared to the younger player? What will they eat, if anything? Will they make any adjustments to their game plan? What type of mental preparation are the players using to stay focused?

During a rain delay at the 1998 U.S. Open, we saw two totally different results. Mary Pierce after losing 6-1 in the first set against Venus Williams fought her heart out in the second. Although she lost the match, she used the time to regroup. The veteran did her best to adjust. Marat Safin, a younger player, did not fair well against Pete Sampras after the weather delay. He appeared to be edgy and lacking focus. The veteran Sampras certainly was better equipped to handle the delay.

The one certainty in life is there will be rough weather. The route to success is never as we plan. There are changes and delays that can affect the outcome. People love to talk about the weather. Weather like life cannot be changed. You do not have to be a veteran to use these delays to your advantage. Preparation, focus, and adaptability are not the possessions of veterans.

Whether it is a business deal or family event, changes do not have to knock us off our game plan. Never allow the external issues to challenge your ability to focus. Concentrate on what you do well and execute on your game plan. Capitalize on the opportunity to regroup. Players expect weather problems. With the proper mental preparation and focus, we can all learn to capitalize on life's delays. Weather it out! It is only water and the next challenge is the best towel.

17

JUST GET IT IN

JUST GET IT IN

There was a nine-year-old boy who simply loved to play tennis. This young man would work very hard each week to improve his skills. He was and still is a coach's dream. Whatever part of the game he is being taught, this boy tries his best to follow the instruction his coach imparts to him. Above all, the young man is patient beyond his years and refuses to take the easy way and push even a point. The lesson of his serve will illustrate for you my reason for sharing his story.

While learning to serve, he struggled to get the serve in the box. His serve would most often be outside the service box or in the net. He lost more matches than he won. His partners in doubles would plead with him to just get the serve in. "Come on, just get it in," they would yell. Not this kid, he stuck to his lessons and concentrated on serving the way he was coached. He continued to lose much more than he won. There was no way this young player was going to be a pusher.

We all face the same pressure as the young man in my story. There is always the temptation to just get it in. Or, to do enough to just get by in our endeavors. We know in our hearts our performance was not our best game, but it was sufficient to get by. There are always partners or colleagues who wish to take the easy path. They plead with us to take short cuts and just get it in. "In" can vary from a project deadline to ethics and values. We conveniently forget the way we were coached and become professional "pushers" attempting to finish the job no matter how ugly the results.

Today, the boy in my story is twelve years old. In his first season of playing USTA Junior tournaments, he won three of the four tournaments he entered. Many of the players who challenged him took the easy path and no longer play tennis. He has become one of the top junior players at his local tennis club. By the way, his serve has become a true weapon.

I think about this young man when I face a professional challenge. It is tempting to just get it in and forget the professional process. We all know people who always take the short cut and rarely learn the right way to get it in. If we concentrate on doing our job the correct way, we will find that we win more than we lose. I think of this young player whenever I consider just getting it in.

18

ON THE SURFACE

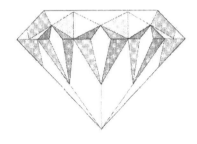

ON THE SURFACE

Professional tennis players are accustomed to competing on different surfaces. Most of the tournaments are played on hardcourt. Hardcourts are considered to be a medium surface allowing for an aggressive style of play. Because it is faster than clay and slower than grass, it permits players from both areas of expertise to compete somewhat equally. Regardless of a player's specialty, with hardcourt they can rely on the consistent bounce of the ball. A hardcourt is smooth with predictable shot outcome.

In life, we try hard to keep our personal "court" smooth. It can be the tennis player relying only on their power game. The businessman refusing the responsibility to mentor a businesswoman. We often fail to reach a new level of achievement because we fear the "surface" of the new responsibility. We should consider using education and experience to prepare our surface for victory. We develop an area of expertise in order to establish a position of strength. We can even become a recognized authority on a particular life surface.

On the surface, we appear to be in control. There is one major problem. The bounce on the surface of life. Real life bounces are inconsistent. They are influenced by variables such as character and reputation. I have always given more attention to my character than my reputation. Reputation lacks fact and can be created from myth. Character is ours to control and develop. The more "surfaces" of life I have played on, the more I have become aware of my responsibility to achieve.

**The truly great player makes character practice
every day and leaves reputation in the locker room.**

As parents and professionals, we all need to keep our surface under
construction. Children will learn to achieve if they see their parents
striving to do the same. It can be a single mother that decides to
take a college course in the evening. Her child will witness her
sacrifice and someday remember their mother when they need to
learn to play on their new surface of life.

If we establish ourselves on different surfaces, our record will
improve. Our record as a parent, professional and humanitarian
will be a winning record. When we compete on a new surface, the
result is always in question. The bounce may be unpredictable, but
the speed of change will never intimidate us.

19

THERE ARE NO UPSETS

THERE ARE NO UPSETS

Humility prevents the underdog from speaking the truth in victory. When they are asked, "How does it feel to win as the underdog?" They smile to themselves. They know there is no such thing as an upset. People would be more forgiving of the favorite in defeat if they understood the power of the underdog moving forward and fearing retreat.

Look at the tennis professional everyone wrote off to age or injury that defeats the stronger opponent. The executive that is overmatched by the more powerful competitor yet secures the deal. Or the child that is labeled a behavioral problem and achieves to their full potential. They all had the vision to move forward and forget the pain of retreat.

Whether you are an athlete, executive or youngster, we all have the same arsenal of weapons to win. Courage, determination, preparation, and faith. The courage to face defeat before the game even begins. The determination to break from the boundaries placed on us by others. The preparation given to us by great parents, coaches and business leaders. And, the faith in our own human spirit.

We place number rankings on athletes, titles on business professionals, and mental health labels on troubled kids. All these are stages for upset. We should achieve by courage not by permission.

Graf returns from injuries, Seles from tragedy, an executive from failed business opportunities, and a child from abuse and neglect. How can they do it? Because they were never underdogs. They were always winners in their own hearts and minds.

The world is full of examples of those that refused to ask permission. Single mothers that raise their children to achieve. Non-profit professionals that sacrifice money for mission. Business leaders with purpose and vision. Each of them a competitor that knows how to play hurt.

If we all seek to find the winner in ourselves, how can there ever be an upset? When others may think we lost, we knew that the competition was a time to learn. As we return to victory, others see an upset. The forehand winner, the signature on the successful business contract or the academic scholarship may appear to spectators as defining moments in the match. But, we the winners realize that victory came from a lifetime of preparing for the pinnacle of challenge.

We knew on that particular court, deal or life moment that the student had become the teacher. If we attack life as a player versus a spectator, we will understand there are no upsets.

20

ENDURANCE

ENDURANCE

E ndurance plays a major role in both sports and business. The business professional building a successful clientele is similar to a tennis player engaged in a major tournament. The player and businessperson may find the going easier in the beginning of the competition. The first week of the tournament can be compared to the early stage of a landing a new customer. At the start, the match or the business strategy may be simple and routine. The difficulty and need for endurance heat up when competitors in sport or business make the first cut. The more deals and matches we enter the more endurance we build for the final week of competition.

The second week of any tournament becomes survival of the fittest. Mental strength is as important as the physical to defeat isolation and self doubt. A champion will tell you that the closer their chance at challenge, the more conscience they become of the fragile opportunity. Mental and physical endurance are the weapons of the leader. All leaders deal with self-doubt and isolation. Difficult decisions can weaken our endurance. Pressure can cause us to lose our focus and become fearful of competition. As leaders, we should increase our endurance by practicing with tough and driven colleagues.

A professional in sports or business builds endurance through activity and sustaining long-term challenges.

In tennis, we have sparring partners that practice with players. In business, it creates little advantage to constantly interact with weak colleagues. They will stifle your ability to grow and compete in the tougher arena. Find professional sparring partners in order to strengthen your performance. Endurance finds it's disciples among the strong and those willing to try what others consider the impossible. In tennis or business, go for the impossible shot. In time and with increased endurance, you will make the impossible the routine.

Practice may produce muscle memory for the player, but endurance produces mental memory for the leader. The memory of what it feels to be a great leader. When others begin to fade, the person with the passion, heart, and courage will endure.

21

RETURN ON INVESTMENT

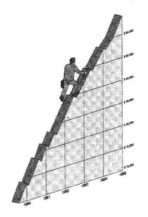

RETURN ON INVESTMENT

All my life I have made investments in the lives of my players. Often, I have not been paid adequately for the service I have provided. I have watched young players turn into professional athletes and turn away from their heritage as role models. They are among the highest paid athletes in the world. They seem to forget their obligation as a role model. My colleagues and family question my return on investment. It is not easy for my friends and family to watch these players forget their mission and vision.

Whether our role is parent or professional, we all make an investment in those around us. The investment in the client, player or child that we strive to support and serve. We make an investment to improve their bottom-line of success. Many times the return on our investment is well below our expectations. There are many that believe I should care more about the bottom-line. They say I should be paid more for my services and advice. My greatest return on investment is the investment I make every day in myself.

Expect little in return for your investment in other people. Open your eyes and see that the true return on investment is the net gain of the improvement in yourself. The most powerful force in the world is the inner energy you possess. We all feel the disappointment when the people we invest in come up short on their responsibility. Parents have their hearts broken over children that stray from their gifts and talents. Executives fear the future when a client they have served leaves for their competitor. I go full out for every player or person in my charge. The investment I make is in my own work ethic and values.

**Invest in your personal goal portfolio.
Your dreams are the worksheet that create
a profitable bottom-line to success.**

I believe that the true return on investment comes when we challenge others to pay their debt to their talents. Talent comes with a price and a premium. The price is to return to those less fortunate our time and attention. A player should not walk away from a child looking for an autograph. Imagine a player taking a moment to stand with the children and give a message about personal potential. Those few words mean more than a hundred autographs. The premium is to remember those that invested their inner energy, so we could triumph over our challenges.

In corporations, the return on investment usually means a financial profit. If you truly dedicate yourself to give more than you get, the return is a profit that grows larger with your commitment to hard work. I have learned that people will leave you and goals will come up short. Never leave yourself and always give your dreams a chance to become someone's reality. Become an investor in your goals and an owner of your dreams. The return on investment is the example you set for everyone following your lead.

22

THE HUNTERS

THE HUNTERS

Successful leaders are the modern day hunters. Every goal and aspiration is a planned hunt to capture the elusive prey. The prey I refer to is the animal that lies in all of us. The animal we all call adversity. Adversity can quietly enter our camp and destroy our map to success.

I have witnessed many players over the years with exceptional raw talent. They were on the hunt to victory. Then, before they could master their new frontier, adversity attacked their base of operations. They started spending more time discussing how adversity developed than solving the problems adversity created.

We should teach people of all ages to think and plan. Planning is what helps a child deal with the unfamiliar. They will make better decisions for their survival and success. They will learn to avoid dangerous pitfalls in their "wilderness".

Many of the young people I see starting their careers are not equipped to handle the unfamiliar and unknown. We, the experienced hunters, should mentor them in how to blaze a trail in life. Teach them to embrace adversity as an opportunity to learn. They will learn to move quietly through adversity by seeing the light in the forest of success.

A visionary is a hunter who can see the future, trap adversity, and track the path to achievement.

As parents, we can teach our children to live with adversity. Then instead of leaving home, they will find their way home. We as mentors need to stop worrying about our survival. We need to stop feeling sorry for ourselves because we chose the wrong path and were lost for a while. Do not panic; you will survive. Whether they are nine or ninety, look for that lost child. Be a skilled hunter and show them the way home.

In my life, there have been times when I felt lost and off the path. I never gave up my focus on my goals and dreams. Sure, I have had setbacks, but my energy and desire to achieve served as my compass to navigate the forest of adversity. Today, those of us that have mapped the tough lands and hunted the crafty challenges are guides for the others.

We have a responsibility as guides to prepare those we take on the hunt. They need to be prepared for the rough weather of goal setting. They should understand that the road to success is filled with adversity and self doubt. On the hunt, they learn to make sacrifices in order to meet the hardship of challenge. Above all, we the guides, remind them that with the end of each hunt, another hunt has just begun.

23

CLIENT – TELL

CLIENT – TELL

I always believed that clientele should be spelled client-tell. It is impossible to serve your clients if they refuse to tell you what they need. Over the years, I have dealt with players that had severe attitude problems. Before you can counsel and coach someone through their problems, they need to open up and discuss their concerns. I know a great deal about coaching, but I never professed to be a mind reader.

People we serve can wander away because they feel we should know what they're thinking and feeling. If we miss any of their cues, they become distant and upset. I consider myself a letter writer. I use letters to my players to get them to concentrate and become motivated. There were times in my past when I should have spoken first and written second. I realized later that I should have given verbal feedback to encourage maximum interaction.

Imagine going to see your doctor regarding a pain in your back. When the physician asks you what is wrong, you respond by telling her to figure it out without tests or patient feedback. There is no way the physician can treat you without your input. Our professional hands are tied without the constant feedback from our clients or players. When we have been in a long-term relationship, we sometime expect our needs to be understood without communication.

The formation of personal potential begins with the ability to communicate.

Client - tell is the structure necessary to build professional partnerships. Through quality interaction, we have the opportunity to achieve goals and dreams. There is not anyone who can be totally successful without the support of others. How often do you remember to thank your colleagues and families for the role they play in your success?

At the Academy, I have been fortunate to surround myself with mostly positive people. When we have a tough day, we communicate our strategy and plan to overcome the obstacles. The same is true in business and family. There will always be difficult days. How we choose to deal with them is the real issue. Hiding our feelings and emotions behind title or position is the framework for failure.

Client-tell can have the same effect on both the leader and the client or player. Many leaders feel that they have no one they can trust to share their personal concerns. As leaders, we should have the courage to tell our colleagues the obstacles we face. Discuss our fears and apprehension. Communication begins at the top and flows through the organization and the family. Silence is golden only when mining fools gold.

24

THE LONG "WEAK"END

THE LONG "WEAK"END

Weekends and holidays are important to refresh ourselves. If however, we stray from our daily routine, we can suffer from the "weak"end. Our routine of practice and work can be reduced, but never eliminated. If we rest for too long a time, our creativity can suffer. Although a player would like a long weekend, they realize the importance of routine.

Leaders who consistently deliver a professional performance are in a zone. They rarely jeopardize their zone for comfort. A strong player or leader often finds relaxation in building new zones where they can achieve. What appears as hard work to others really is rest to the overachiever.

Often, when people return from a holiday, they waste an entire day before they become productive. While at rest, overachievers are planning and creating an enhanced system of success. They visualize themselves in a new arena. When they return from their rest, they possess a plan to improve. They are refreshed, relaxed, and ready to attack new challenges.

In the fast paced world we live, taking a break can be difficult. We need time to create not just concentrate. We can all rest from our normal routine. There will never be a "weak"end if we rob routine to build a new system of energy. All the great players and leaders will tell you that practice is sacred. The religion of reaching our full potential comes from the ability to build while we rest.

25

EXPECTATION

EXPECTATION

Unrealistic expectation can be the toughest player in the draw. There are so many expectations placed on the competitors in a tournament. It can become difficult for the players to keep a realistic perspective. They need to evaluate the expectation that is being placed on them and determine if it is truly realistic. The same applies to children and professionals in any arena. Often, we give less than our best performance because we were expected to win.

When dealing with other's expectations, we are often faced with issues that force us out of our game plan. The experts that thought the player should win in straight sets. The parent that expects nothing but straight A's or the board of directors that expects another straight quarter of large profits. Many times we abandon our vision, and motivation, because other's expectations are either too high or too low.

The only expectation that is reliable is to do our best. Whether on the tennis court, classroom or boardroom, expect to make your own breaks. Believe in your instinct not your press. All competitors expect to win. But, the great players expect only to battle to the end. We should teach our children and our colleagues to expect a battle in every challenge. Expectation can be the Achilles heel of anyone who competes in life. The truth is that the victor often expects nothing but the best from themselves.

26

CROWDED IN

CROWDED IN

A tennis crowd can impact the outcome of a match. For or against a player, the crowd can be the largest reason for a loss of concentration. The crowd can distract the player's focus and ability to concentrate. Players may have an easier time reading opponents than the reaction of the crowd.

The player may be confused why they are treated like the enemy. Often, the crowd will change their support because they want the match to be extended. History is filled with players that battled against the crowd and their opponents to victory. There are also an equal number of players that rode to victory on the voices of a supportive crowd.

Every day we all face the crowd. The crowd may be our customers or our employees. Many factors determine whether they are for or against us. Many people fear success and failure with equal weight. Overachievers have the ability to concentrate whether they receive silence or applause. With the crowd behind them, an exhausted competitor can find new energy. Alone a player can become frustrated and take excessive risks.

You should never fear the crowd reaction. Great leaders play for themselves. They listen for the roar of personal achievement. They are a crowd of one.

You can take the crowd out of the competition. Stay focused and be sincere to your plan. Go to the edge of risk and reward where no crowd exists. Look up and all you will see are the faces of followers. Followers that wished they could go to the edge with you. In the end, the crowd will stand and cheer the warrior who refuses to surrender their edge.

27

NO EXCUSE

NO EXCUSE

I have lost my share of clients and deals. I considered them as opportunities to learn and teach. The one behavior that is impossible for me to tolerate is loss by excuse. We all know the players or professionals that have an excuse to explain defeat. Rarely do they see their personal performance as the root cause of their loss.

If you want to watch excuse building in the formative stage, observe young players. Often, when they lose a match, they have the reason ready to deliver. Excuses range from my arm hurts to the racquet tension is incorrect. The player that defeated them is robbed of the reality of true victory. Between competitors, there must be honest closure when their hands meet at the net.

The pretender has their excuse ready before the competition. Contenders have no excuse; they grow stronger from battle.

My experience has taught me that there are players that prepare their excuses long before the match has started. They are not true fighters preparing to win the competition. They are doubting participants preparing to justify loss. We can see it clearer in sports, but the use of excuse is prevalent in all areas of life. Business or personal excuse building robs you of increasing your skill package.

Consider the marketing professional that plans their excuse before ever delivering their proposal to the client. They are ready with their excuse if the price is too high or the service insufficient. Instead of concentrating on their sales skills and customer needs, they focus on the possibility of failure. We could all be better at time management if we concentrate less on excuse management. There are only so many excuses available to the excuse giver. Eventually, people see excuses for what they actually represent. An excuse is discovered to be nothing more than a lie.

If we stand as role models, we crush excuse and build honor. Children learn from watching our behavior. They remember the player that throws their racquet or tanks a match. They quietly observe the use of excuse from their parents, teachers and friends. We generate the validity that excuses are natural and adult approved.

Excuses are a sign of weakness. Strength comes from admitting defeat and building on the experience. I refuse to make excuses a part of my being. When you are free of the excuse baggage, you can travel faster and lighter to your sure victories. Experience the thrill of open competition. Fly full speed to your goals and dreams. Kick excuse out of your equipment bag. Carry your courage and honesty to the matches of life.

28

AFTER THE TOSS

AFTER THE TOSS

The time approaches for the finals of a tournament. After two weeks of intense competition, we arrive at the defining moment. The last matches are decided when one of the players lifts the ball for the final toss. All the matches and all the drama are decided on the final toss that will determine championship point.

The camera crews have captured the matches for all time. The players realize that their movements and mannerisms whether foolproof or foolhardy will forever be on tape. Imagine if all of us were video taped in our life's competition. The businessperson taped as they deliver their presentation to their client. The parent as they interact with their children. The accountability factor would definitely alter our delivery on the world court.

A professional tennis player knows the pressure of competition and the accountabilities to millions of viewers present and future. At every tournament, the ultimate match is truly waged between the same two competitors. They are named character and reputation. Character is who we are and reputation is what others think we are. After the final toss, we are left to confront both of them.

UNDER CONSTRUCTION

The truly great player makes character practice every day and leaves reputation in the locker room. After the final toss, the player may lose the match, but the champion leaves carried on the shoulders of character. We have little control over reputation. Reputation lacks fact and can be created from myth. Character is ours to control and develop. After your final toss is lifted and the point is over, move to the next match. Character is ready for the next challenger. Character always has an aura of invincibility. Before and after the toss, character fears no opponent.

29

THE FINAL TIEBREAK

THE FINAL TIEBREAK

A tiebreaker can be exciting and packed with pressure. The player who was close to winning the set cannot believe they are in a tiebreaker. They may lose their mental edge and, therefore, the match. In a tiebreaker, the player needs all their weapons to function at a high level. There is no room for error and little time for adjustment. The player to serve first often has the advantage and wins the first three points.

We spend the majority of our life in a tiebreaker. When we think we have achieved an advantage, an opponent closes on our lead. In business, the minute we build a better product or service, the competition quickly recovers to counter. We counsel our children on the latest hazards only for a new danger to develop.

Like a tennis player, we can control the pressure of the tiebreaker. No matter how we plan and prepare, will eventually face our tiebreaker. We should stay mentally tough and concentrate on the point not the process. We should never spend time debating how we arrived to a tiebreaker, but focus on the strategy to win.

Like a tennis tiebreaker, the first three points are critical. The first point is to maintain our character. The second point is to focus on integrity. The third point is the power of our conviction. We will find victory if we serve to others and not only ourselves. If others duplicate our style of play, then we truly won the final tiebreaker.

30

THE LAST BELL

THE LAST BELL

The bell at the end of the school day is really a wake up call to the rest of your life. When the school bell sounds, be ready to achieve your goals. Use your education to help yourself and your families have a better life.

**The school bell is the starting gun for your race
to personal achievement.**

The final bell announces more than just the end of school. It reminds us to prepare for the challenges we will face when we leave school. Doing well in school helps us prepare for those challenges.

If you watch a professional fight, there is a term called saved by the bell. It means that a fighter might have been knocked out if the bell had not ended the round. The ring bell saved the fighter from losing the fight. The fighter has a second chance to recover before the bell sounds to continue the fight.

You are just like a professional fighter. School trains you with the skills to fight any obstacle in life. The school bell can save you by giving you the knowledge you need to win your fights in life. Education teaches you to move fast and solve problems. Education is your fight trainer to take on the tougher opponent.

Just like a fighter, education gives you the power to punch harder at your dreams. School teaches you to take a punch when a problem hits you. Life requires that you learn to fight for your goals. Education can turn a small unknown fighter into a great and powerful leader. Do well in school and you will be undefeated in your fight to achieve your full potential. School is your wake up call to begin your quest to new challenges and excitement.

Your tough opponent may be getting a good job. Being able to read directions and follow instructions. Education gives you the ability to travel and speak to people from all over the world. Education rings the bell that leads you from grade school to greatness.

Whether you are an adult or child, education is the platform to launch your goal package. We are all constantly learning as we continue on our personal path to achievement. The moment we cease to learn new systems and processes we begin the decline to certain failure. Always believe, regardless of your age, that each morning you are on your way to school. The world is our classroom; pay attention and you will sit at the head of the class.

31

ON THE EDGE

ON THE EDGE

Apparently, luck was high on Napoleon's resume requirements. For a small explosive Italian man, he knew the importance of surrounding himself with forces of spirit and accomplishment.

The following story is told about Napoleon. While discussing a particular general in command of his troops on the eastern front he was told by a confidant of the virtues of this general's tactical abilities. It is reported that Napoleon cut him short saying, "I don't want to know how good he is. I know he's good. If he weren't good, he wouldn't be a general. I want to know, is he lucky?"

Luck follows skill closely, which is the result when you surround yourself with the smartest and most talented men and women in your world.

Like winning a championship, it is an ideal that is not always easy to attain, but undoubtedly worth the effort. Sure, it's even easy enough to find the talent. What's difficult is finding the courage to lead those you know are more talented or instinctively smarter.

First time jitters not withstanding, most people never feel comfortable in an inferior world. Those who do are either fooling themselves or going nowhere waiting for a train at the bus stop. In an inferior world, inevitably there are considerations of pride, to say nothing of ego. Napoleon's thoughts on fear were "he who fears being conquered, is sure of defeat." We have to hire people smarter than us. Yet, knowing how intimidating intelligence, ability, and gusto can be, we may tend to be reluctant.

Insecurities boosted by reluctance are experiences each of us has more often than we care to admit. The failure of admission is the first mistake. We are not all equally gifted. At least not in all the same areas. However, we are all gifted.

The secret is to discover early in life, your special gifts. To polish them until they shine so brightly that you compel your surroundings.

To say that, as young adults, we set aside our fears and did as we suggest would be too charitable. Moreover, while we now know to hire people smarter than ourselves, it took us a long time to be comfortable with them and ourselves.

None of us were great in our early years. Whether we were challenged on a tennis court when bashing balls with the best or negotiating a business deal against a professional hustler, it kept us awake at night. Surely then, our students can't help but notice who's the better player. Once they do, it haunts us because we fear they might leave. You know what? Some do and it makes us more paranoid.

What is anyone to do in such a situation? The only chance at survival is to realize that you need to contract with the best and stay out of the comfort zone. Over the years, I have realized that people fear both success and failure. When asked the question, most people will respond that they are convinced that the fear of failure is greater than the fear of success. But, in reality, both success and failure carry an equal curse. If you seek to find the true essence of leadership, you will see the leader who understands that both success and failure can keep the leader and their colleagues frozen in their comfort zone.

Far too often, we reach our comfort zone because we have obtained a certain pinnacle of success. Whether your world is hiring better coaches than yourself or better salespeople, there is always a fear that we will be surpassed and forgotten.

A lesson in life that has never missed is that if we surround ourselves with great people, we build a platform for success and long-term achievement that lowers the fear factor for everyone.

Look at the business world. The reason that many business leaders fail is due to their fear regarding the mentoring and training of people who are better than them. They are comfortable in their niche and fear being pushed by the overachiever, hungry for success. The leader eventually loses those individuals and is left with "dead wood" employees that eventually destroy the organization. The world is screaming for visionaries. We, as leaders, cannot be futurists if we protect the turf we perceive to belong to us. For the leader, there is no comfort zone if we push to stay on the edge.

32

ON THE LINE

ON THE LINE

Often the momentum of a match can change as the result of a simple line call. Some players can lose their focus because of a call they believe was in error. They allow someone to control their destiny. They let emotion dictate the outcome of the match.

All aspects of life involve line calls. The professional that believes they were passed over for a promotion. The youngster cut from the school team. They permit these "calls" to collapse their dreams. We need to enhance our primary skill package and achieve to our ability. Losing our focus because of life's line calls can leave us bitter and sullen.

Observe how the best players and leaders deal with their line calls. Some use emotion, but only to maintain focus and attack their goal. Other competitors stay calm and burn the internal fire even hotter. They understand bad calls are in every part of life. The wrong reaction keeps us from achieving our goals.

In any challenge we face, we must be prepared for the calls that go against us. We can excel through those moments by reaching deep into our skill package. Line calls always seem to even out. Expect them to be there and you will not be surprised when they appear. When they occur, attack your challenge harder and with more conviction.

33

THE EYES OF A CHILD

THE EYES OF A CHILD

We must never lose the child within us. Successful leaders have an inner child that prevents them from being complacent. They are always at play, changing the rules to fit their next challenge.

In every overachiever, you see the eyes of a playful child with the intensity of a focused professional.

We should all view photos of ourselves from different ages. Try placing the photographs in front of you starting from the youngest age to the most current year. Look at your eyes. Do they still have that fire and desire to play? Our eyes, it has been said, are the windows to our soul. Whether we are coaches, parents, players or business leaders, together we should build the playground of life. The playground is always open to these children of challenge to play and achieve their goals.

Wherever we stand is our playground.
Whatever we dream is our game.

Children will always play with other children regardless of race or religion. If a child can look into our eyes and see another child, they will always follow us to their goals and dreams. After all is said and done, isn't life just a game? And, who better to play a game than a leader with the spirit of a child.

137

Children are often fearless. They try different things because they believe they can accomplish every goal they attempt. They look at pessimists with a strange and confused look. They wonder why someone would speak of defeat prior to the start of the game. We hear people talk about adults as role models for children. Perhaps, children can serve as role models for adults.

Many of the great players I have coached refused to lose the child that first fell in love with the game. There are those that started with me at a very young age. Decades later, I see them at a match or event and I still hear the child speaking to me. Their energy and vision remains at the childlike high they had when I first coached them as young players.

My youth is my most priceless possession. It has allowed me to move off a particular failure to find and achieve a success. A child hustles from one playground to the other. We should learn to hustle from one goal to another. If you are looking to form a board of directors, visit your local playground. Witness the energy and excitement of the children and recruit for your board starting with those qualities.

The eyes of a child are the message center to the soul of achievement. Enjoy the game and never regret the result. Continue to seek new playmates that possess the drive and determination to never take you or themselves too seriously.

34

THE TANK IS EMPTY

THE TANK IS EMPTY

Most sport fans can relate an event where they witnessed a player tank a competition. You may be surprised to know that often the player believes that they were doing their best to win, even though it appears to everyone watching that they tanked. Tanking can be an unplanned, unconscious reaction in the face of competition.

I have had players be completely unaware that they were tanking a match. Tanking leaves one with an empty feeling because it causes the player to be confused by the results. The player truly believes they left everything they had on the court. When others express their opinion that the player tanked, the player is confused. Tanking was never their intent.

Tanking is not always unintentional. Some individuals fear both success and failure. They set their goals too low and when faced with advancement tank their future. Tanking is not restricted to athletes. Parents may tank when their families are faced with new challenges they believe are outside their skill package.

At the academy, families are often faced with the decision to allow their child to reside at the academy on a full time basis. Even though they support their child's decision to live at the academy, their actions may unintentionally send a different message.

**Every difficult decision in life has the potential for tanking.
Tanking is prevented when we do our best to deliver
our potential. Losing, if we do our best,
deserves the same respect as winning.**

Even the best parents can tank for a period of time. They may temporary lose their children to the wrong crowd or environment. They try everything to help their child through the difficult moments. When the child stays on the wrong road, the parents may feel helpless and give up on the fight. Thus, tanking.

Business professionals can also be victims of tanking. They may feel they did not deserve the deal. They may be unable to see themselves as peers of their clients. The older adversary battling for the new client may intimidate the young professional. Tanking has one true cure. A dedicated coach who understands the pitfalls and the signals of tanking. Players have their coaches, children have their parents, and professionals have their mentors.

We will all eventually face the moment where tanking is an option. If we stay dedicated to our values and strive to do our best, our tank will never be empty. We can step from the arena and know we gave all we had.

35

TOP RANKING

TOP RANKING

I have had the privilege to coach greatness. Players who had the ability to be the best. Arguably, Pete Sampras is one of the greatest to ever play the game of tennis. He is a role model for champions of all walks of life.

Even when you're the best like Pete Sampras, there is still the temptation to take the easy path. Everyday, our nation's children suffer from the wrong role models being marketed to them. It is believed that Pete does not have that media flash. What better role model than Pete to represent the sport? After all, the ranking of number one in life must stand for more than match records. It should stand for life rankings. In the end, tennis history will record Pete's match records, but his character and courage will follow him into his life choices after tennis.

Throughout our nation, there are non-profit providers of human services that are exactly the courageous comparison to Pete Sampras. These professionals that serve clients are constantly tempted to take the easier path. They are modest and reluctant to market their successes. Yet, in these professionals are the role models for life. They are the professionals that try to reverse the damage caused by society and years of children choosing the wrong role models.

In a world where profit and perks often dominate the decisions of our athletes and professionals, these non-profit professionals concentrate on service. Most are underpaid and overworked. They concentrate and focus on the issues of society that many of us wish to forget. The abuse directed at our youth and elderly continues to

145

escalate. These non-profit professionals are the guardians of the disadvantaged.

The non-profit organizations are rarely the media darlings. They wait in the background ready to assist all of humanity that is troubled. There are times when our athletes become the wrong role models for children. Our professional athletes should reach out to our nation's non-profit organizations. Donate time at these facilities motivating the staff, as well as, the residents. The character and courage of both our athletes and non-profit professionals would set the standard for the role model of the future.

In 1999, I received an award at the National Symposium for Children and Poverty. It was one of the most exciting moments of my career. I met the men and women who dedicate their careers and lives to serving the youth of America. They have my support and respect.

Our human service agencies are full of kids many try to forget. But, we as a society created them and we must take the responsibility of caring for them. Character and courage can be taught, as long as, we are patient for their long-term reward. That reward is the healing of America's children.

36

HOCUS FOCUS

HOCUS FOCUS

The ability to remain focused on the task in front of you is the key to generating the power to sustain momentum. In my career as a coach, I have witnessed players with exceptional ability lose because they lost concentration and focus. In a close match, the first player to lose focus will most definitely lose the edge. Momentum can shift with the loss of focus magic. Many of the great players focus differently to achieve the necessary results.

Monica Seles for the most part kept her focus within the playing surface and the tennis ball. It was unusual to see her eyes drift to the outside, even to see her family and coaches. John McEnroe throughout his matches would argue almost everything. Statistics have shown that he was able to focus on the ball right after these outbursts and win eighty percent of the points. Many of his opponents felt he did this to break their focus and intensity.

There are those who confuse focus with intensity. Focus is a consistent pressure applied to the task or objective. Intensity is a hot burn used like a retrorocket to move to the next level.

Intensity without focus will neutralize creativity.

As a coach, I often feel like a magician. I may suggest a player adjust their grip and "presto" like magic they are hitting winners. I search for the magic to levitate my player to the next level. When we focus and concentrate, we produce successful results.

We all possess the ability to pull a large success from our magician's hat of skills. The hocus focus magic wand may be our tennis racquet, golf club, pen or science homework. Our life's spectators are seeing a magic act performed right before their eyes. The magic of our mind is focusing on its objective.

I believe a parent focused on their family or a professional focused on their business objectives creates magic. Attempt to always stay focused on the results. Visualize yourself succeeding at your best. Share your plan with colleagues. Seek the wisdom of those you trust to give you an honest answer. Be a role model of concentration and determination for others.

Hocus focus gives off the illusion of magic, but in reality it is driven by the desire to be the best. If you focus on your dreams, I assure you the hand of success will be quicker than the eye of defeat.

37

FOREVER A COACH

FOREVER A COACH

Throughout more than four decades of coaching, I have interacted with people from all walks of life. After all my experiences, I certainly know a coach when I meet one. Many of the best coaches I know are not always from the world of sports. They are parents, business leaders, and others that coach their children and colleagues to achieve to their potential. The game may change for all of us, but one truth is eternal; we are forever coaches.

Successful coaches have the capacity to elevate the performance of a student to another level. All a coach can hope to achieve is to elevate the student to reach the maximum level of their ability. Trust me, this is not an easy thing to do! A coach must understand their students needs, moods, and fears. A priority is to gain the respect of their student. Indeed, this may be the defining characteristic of a coach. A coach goes beyond the boundary often set for an instructor or teacher. A coach develops an understanding of the true personality and other hidden nuances of their student. The history books are filled with talented players that failed because they took to the road of challenge without a coach.

A true coach establishes a bond of trust that is similar to a parent. It is the same with a professional sales manager or other business coaching teams. Parents must seek to understand their children's needs and personality. If we coach from our needs and not our student, we eventually jeopardize the success of both the coach and student.

The best coaches have the ability to push a student to reach limits. Limits that in many cases, the students didn't know they were capable of achieving. These coaches must recognize the moment when they have extracted all that is available from their student or colleague. Some coaches push beyond this level. Trouble for student and coach is not far behind.

Trouble can be avoided if you have a strategy for coaching. The great Australian coach Harry Hopman won more Davis Cup matches than any other coach in history. Harry had the simplest strategy known to man. Work harder than your opponent does before you get on the court. It was sweet, simple and ahead of its time. Harry planned and Harry executed and that made him a winner and forever a coach.

The interaction of coach and student is like a mirror.
A mirror that reflects the strengths and weaknesses of both.

As a parent, motivator, or coach make a firm commitment to go the distance. Never overlook anything for your protégé. Develop your personal coaching style. A coaching style that represents your beliefs and values. Your coaching style is your brand. A brand that will label your legacy as forever a coach who cared. A coach who cared about their student and their mission.

38

ALL IN THE PLAN

ALL IN THE PLAN

J ust as you would never enter a sales meeting without a plan, a player should never enter a tennis match without a plan. The plan may be as simple as hitting every ball to the backhand or as intricate as coming in on your serve and attacking a certain area of the court.

There are parallels between sports planning and how it relates to your business, home, or family relationships. Before the Academy's full-time tennis program begins, each day thirty tennis pros lock themselves in a room and create the day's program. Obviously, a master plan is in effect and the daily meeting is simply a way of making sure all eventualities are covered.

To live comfortably in today's world, more often than not, requires the income of two parents. Families whose children attend afternoon activities require planning, coordination, and assistance. This is no different than tennis. Planning is defining a strategy that can get you from one point to another. In tennis, that point is winning. We tell our students and coaches, "Make a plan, then work the plan." The same applies to parenting, and with luck, success will be around the corner.

Planning is the palm reading of success. With the proper amount of planning, you can eliminate the need for a crystal ball. The future is never in doubt.

There are many lessons on the court, which transcend the court. One of the most obvious is "mood swings." On the court, as in life, mood swings usually parallel momentum. Positive and negative attitudes affect more than just hitting a ball across the net, they affect associates and projects. On the court, we teach keeping emotions, even under the difficult circumstances, to stay positive. Control your emotions and the chances you will control the court are greatly enhanced.

It's the same in life. Nothing is more difficult than competing against someone who is always positive and who exude confidence. In the boardroom, a positive professional controls the momentum of the project and its results.

Often a person will ask for a plan and a strategy to succeed in their endeavor. Those who ask are usually looking for a secret weapon. There are none. A plan must be created through practice and knowing your ability. We should set ourselves against both the opponent and our own limitations. When we follow the plan, we can make adjustments that offset the unexpected changes in the match or life challenges.

Most corporations do not plan properly. They set their long-range plans too short. Most view long-range as three to five years. I suggest you plan for as far as you can see. Your plan and your vision are teammates. Allow both to travel as far ahead as possible.

39

THE LAST HANDSHAKE

THE LAST HANDSHAKE

Over the years there have been many memorable handshakes after great matches. If you look closely, you will see the power of respect in each of those handshakes. The handshake combinations are in themselves the signature of this great competition. The handshakes at the net, with the chair referee, spectators in the stands, ball boys and girls, and the fans at home symbolize the energy.

When match point is declared, witness the respect at the net. Some players look first to the crowd. Others seek to find a family member or coach. Then, there are the combatants that look first to their worthy opponent. They move to the last handshake and then to the celebration. Within that handshake, lies the memory of the competition. The memories of the anticipation, expectation, determination, and dedication of these great warriors locked in battle.

We have attempted to connect the world of tennis to the matches of life. We believe that we all have competitions that bring us to the last handshake. Regardless the outcome, we must show respect at the net. We are the role models for our families, colleagues, and friends. Someone is always watching how we choose to handle victory and defeat.

With focus and determination, we can all become leaders. We all have our areas of professionalism and expertise. Together we stand each day on the world court. Never fear the bad bounce, the poor line call, or the stronger opponent. There will be bad weather and hostile crowds. Our strings will break and the surface will be too fast. We will work alone and in teams. In the end, it is our character and heart that will win the match. The last handshake will forever be about respect and the opportunity to compete.

40

THE LAST BALL

THE LAST BALL

I'm frequently asked, "Nick, is this your last attempt to take one of your students to the top? Your last attempt to write the definitive book on tennis? Your last attempt to secure your name in the history books forever?" The truth is, like the rest of us, I don't know if it's my last of "anything." I do know that in order to be successful you can never stop trying. That doesn't mean you can't hit your "last ball" in one endeavor and begin another.

Our sport is replete with players who have reached the pinnacle of success only to forge new and equally successful adventures. My good friend Arthur Ashe, following his on-court success, turned his attention to helping inner city children. Long after his untimely death, the Ashe Foundation along with his enduring legacy continues to grace our wonderful sport. No one could ever accuse Arthur of not challenging the "last ball". Stefan Edberg, whose elegance and grace under pressure, distinguished him in a field of distinguished players, always understood the value of the "last ball". As his priorities moved toward his family and the time came for him to leave the game that had meant so much to him, he did so with the elegance that had draped his professional career. I admire and respect Stefan's approach to the "last ball" and, as difficult as it was for him to leave, he handled it his way- with style and grace.

If you think that the challenges of the "last ball" are an easy decision, think again. Even someone as cerebral as Boris Becker has had difficulty with his "last ball". As his retirement evidences, he continues to dabble in the game. Leaving something in which you have written all the records is never easy.

Then, there are the John Glenns of the world. At an age when most people have played their "last ball", Glenn is looking to conquer new heavens. Glenn's achievements, like those of Mother Theresa, whose sole aim was to save "one more child", are remarkable for what they refuse to recognize—that is, someone else's desire to impose limits on their "last ball".

Where does that leave you and I? Dylan Thomas' eulogy for his dying father is a good beginning.

> *"Rage, rage on into that good night,"*

he wrote of his father's last few minutes on earth. I like that because it best epitomizes how I feel. Like you, I do not know what my "last ball" will be, nor is it my place to tell how to handle yours. This much I can assure you. As darkness falls on the last court of my life, with all of my strength I will be running down the "last ball". With luck, I may even hit a winner.

Under Construction – The Seminar

Building the Ultimate Personal And Professional Game

Strike With the Heart of A Professional Athlete And The Savvy of A Business Leader

This institute combines the best from the world of sports and business into models for life-long success. Visionaries, thinkers and leaders crave personal and professional opportunities. They are able to move quickly to the challenges and accept the risk that accompanies the unknown. From the locker room to the family room, the need to change is the essence of creativity. Wherever our path leads us, we should look at change as the opportunity to improve our game.

Nick Bollettieri, President and Founder, Bollettieri Sports Academy
Nick knows how to nurture achievement. He has coached many of today's top twenty tennis players: Andre Agassi, Monica Seles, Brian Gottfried, Jimmy Arias, Paul Annacone, Anna Kournikova, Mary Pierce and Tommy Haas. Hear Nick's tactics and strategies on achieving success in all aspects of your life.

167

Nick believes that we are connected together whether our life experiences come from the boardroom, family room or locker room. Regardless of our personal arena, we are all players in the same game. Whatever our age, eight or eighty, every day we choose our opportunities by our first and last ball.

Personal and professional growth means accepting new challenges and creating exciting opportunities. Growth builds confidence and character. Take a risk and find reward. Challenge yourself to accomplish goals in the most difficult business arenas.

A renowned tennis coach and mentor, Nick is outspoken, passionate, fearless and inspirational. He continues the vision of pioneers like Arthur Ashe to help minority youth. His perspective on personal growth is a presentation you will not forget.

Anthony C. Gruppo, President and Founder, Lehr Management Corporation

It is no longer enough to be busy. We must be productive, animated and energetic in every goal we attempt to accomplish. We have to set a strategy and mission for ourselves, both short and long-term, which keeps us focused on the tasks and challenges that lie ahead.

Anthony believes most leaders fear losing their edge, their effectiveness and perhaps their ability to lead someday. Leadership, marketing and motivation are the keys to one's success. Almost anything is possible if we understand what motivates and makes us successful.

A national marketer and visionary leader, this dynamic presenter, author and motivator challenges you to think in new powerful ways. Anthony shows how to create employee investment in your business by teaching your employees to think and act like owners. Motivating everyone to improve business is a creative tool for organizational expansion.

To learn more about the institute contact Nick or Anthony.

You can reach Nick at 941-755-1000, 800-USA-NICK or www.bollettieri.com OR Anthony at 800-634-8237 or www.anthony.gruppo@hslehr.com

NOTES

59947025R00113

Made in the USA
Middletown, DE
23 December 2017